Who Will Follow Jesus?
Studies to Help Disciples Grow Stronger

by Mark Roberts

© 2018 One Stone Press.
All rights reserved. No part of this book may be reproduced in any form without written permission of the publisher.

Published by:
One Stone Press
979 Lovers Lane
Bowling Green, KY 42103

Printed in the United States of America

ISBN-13: 978-1-941422-38-0

www.onestone.com

Table of Contents

Introduction 5

Lesson 1: Disciples Prioritize 7

Lesson 2: Disciples Pray 15

Lesson 3: Disciples Work Together 21

Lesson 4: Disciples Think and Ask Questions 29

Lesson 5: Disciples Love Others 37

Lesson 6: Disciples Teach Others 43

Lesson 7: Disciples Fail but Never Quit 49

This workbook was written by Mark Roberts, a Christian interested in helping you get a great start in Christianity. Please do not alter this material without written permission from the author. Further, please do not copy or reproduce this material. Contact the publisher to purchase professionally produced books at a very affordable price.

Using This Material

1. Study each lesson carefully. Filling in the blanks and answering the questions in each lesson assists the learning process. Maximize the value of this material by working each lesson before class.

2. Set aside a certain time when you will study the Bible and work in this lesson book. Studying and working without interruption is especially beneficial.

3. Areas with a star beside them (★) represent points that should be given particular attention.

4. Review the past lesson briefly before starting the next lesson.

5. Write any questions or comments in the margins.

6. All Scripture quotations are from the New King James Version.

Introduction

Welcome, new Christian

Congratulations on becoming a Christian. You have turned away from the emptiness and vanity of this world and have determined to find the abundant life that only Jesus offers. Without question, this decision is the most important one you have ever made. Your faith in Christ moved you to repent of sin, to confess Him as the Son of God, and to be immersed in water for the forgiveness of sins. These things will make, for you, an eternity of difference.

But what happens now? Christianity is not a single decision, a one-time event that can be completed and forgotten. No, Christianity is a way of life that is lived on a daily basis. Jesus says: "If anyone desires to come after Me, let him deny himself, and take up his cross daily, and follow Me" (Luke 9:23). You have already expressed your desire to "come after" Jesus. How do you live out that desire each day? What does it mean to "take up a cross?" How do we follow Jesus?

These questions are at the core of the discipleship concept. Jesus did not die so people would go to church on Sunday, practicing Christianity as a kind of weekend hobby. Jesus wants disciples: people who are committed to learning about Him and following Him at all times. The seven lessons in this book are designed specifically to help you effectively begin this process. Each lesson is based on material from the Gospel of Luke, a book that gives a full explanation of following Jesus Christ. Through interaction with the Word of God, this lesson guide, other Christians, and with much prayer you can lay the groundwork for a lifetime of solid, fulfilling discipleship.

Open your heart, open your Bible, and get ready to answer the question of questions: "Who will follow Jesus?"

Welcome, rededicated Christian

Many Christians use this material to rebuild their walk with Jesus Christ after a period of spiritual apathy or even worldliness. If this is what brings you to these lessons, this book can help you.

Usually, we lose our Christianity because we forget the fundamentals that were once so important to us (see Revelation 2:4). To "restart" your spiritual life, you need to rediscover those fundamentals, beginning with the critical issue of genuine discipleship. That is why this book is exactly what you need to begin again with Christ. This material's focus is how to be a follower of Jesus, a disciple. So, although the book will speak occasionally to new Christians, please know that the writer had you in mind too. *Who Will Follow Jesus* invites you to follow Jesus again as never before!

6   Who Will Follow Jesus?

Lesson 1

Disciples Prioritize

   A. What do you want the most? What is your top priority?

   B. "They brought their boats to land, forsook all and followed Him" (Luke 5:11).

      1. A disciple is a learner-follower, one who learns from and follows his master. He does as the master instructs.

      2. Luke 5:11 shows Peter, Andrew, James and John doing this.

      3. They made the same choice that you have made: to be a disciple of Christ.

      4. The expression "forsook all, and followed Him" shows how this decision radically changed their priorities in life.

   C. In this lesson you will learn:

      1. What the disciple's single priority must be.

      2. How the disciple's sole priority affects one's life.

I. What does the disciple want most?

   A. The disciple wants to be like his/her teacher.

      1. Jesus says: "A disciple is not above his _____, but everyone who is perfectly trained will be like his teacher" (Luke 6:40).

      2. Discipleship means becoming like our Master, Jesus: "to be conformed to the image of His Son" (Romans 8:29).

      3. There are many definitions for "religion" or "being religious." Discipleship should not be confused with worldly concepts of religion. Discipleship (Christianity) is the process of becoming like Jesus Christ.

   B. This is the essence of Christianity (discipleship): to become like Jesus.

8   Who Will Follow Jesus?

   1. "To this you were called, because _____ also suffered for us, leaving us an _____, that you should follow His steps." (1 Peter 2:21).

   2. In every situation, in every circumstance, the disciple asks, "How would Jesus act in this situation?," "What would He say?," "What would He do?," or "How can I conduct myself to bring glory to Him?"

   ★ 3. This point is crucial to all spiritual development. Christianity is the process of changing self to be like Christ.

   4. Jesus calls this "following Me:" "If anyone desires to _____ after Me, let him _____ himself, and take up his _____ daily, and follow Me" (Luke 9:23).

   5. Whether it is termed Christianity, following Jesus, or discipleship the meaning is the same: becoming like Jesus.

C. What motivates the disciple to change and become more like Jesus?

   1. The eternal reward of heaven gives the disciple courage, motivation, and endurance to continue discipleship on a daily basis (see 2 Corinthians 4:16-18).

   2. Luke urges the disciple to strive for heaven. He bluntly, but honestly, contrasts the terrors of hell with the joys of heaven.

   3. Read Luke 16:19-31. What was the end result of each man's life? _____
   _____

   4. List the horrors of eternal torment the rich man is enduring:
   _____
   _____

   5. List the glories of heaven that Lazarus is enjoying:
   _____
   _____

   6. Luke's message is obvious: don't miss heaven! What is the only way to get to heaven (see John 14:6)? _____
   _____

LESSON 1 Disciples Prioritize   9

   D. Is heaven the only motivator for Christians?
   1. No. Jesus taught that Christians are winners now, in this life here on earth.
   2. Read John 10:10. What kind of life does Jesus offer His followers now? _____
   _____
   3. Read Philippians 4:11-13. Does Paul sound like an unhappy Christian?_____
   4. Think carefully. How will your Christianity make your life better now? How does becoming like Jesus make you a better spouse, employee, or neighbor? Identify some specific advantages Christians have over those who do not know Jesus: _____
   _____
   _____

   E. Summary: Disciples desire to be like Jesus for two reasons.
   1. Becoming like Christ is the only way to heaven.
   2. Becoming like Christ is the only means to true happiness here on this earth.

II. **How do we "deny self" to be like Jesus?**
   A. The disciple obeys God instead of pleasing self.
   1. Obedience is an attitude of submission to God and compliance with His will in all things.
   2. Every part of life is made to conform to God's will, not our own.
   3. Read Ephesians 4:22-24. Paul says we have "put off" the old man and "put on" the new man. Who controls the new man?
   _____

   ★ 4. The essence of obedience is submission. Read Luke 5:4-5.
      a. Did Peter want to go fishing again? _____
      b. Did Peter think he would catch anything? _____
      c. Why did Peter go fishing anyway?_____
      _____

    d. What does this teach us about obeying Jesus even when we do not understand or agree with His commands?
    _____
    _____

 5. Obedience is the test of our discipleship: "But why do you call _____ 'Lord, Lord,' and do not _____ the things which I _____?" (Luke 6:46)
 6. If we truly love God and His Son, obedience will be our way of life: "If you _____ Me, keep _____ commandments" (John 14:15).
 7. We deny self to be like Jesus by obeying Him and His word.

B. The disciple obeys Jesus, even if family is opposed to it.
 1. "If anyone comes to Me and does not _____ his father and mother, wife and children, brothers and sisters, yes, and his _____ life also, he cannot be My _____" (Luke 14:26).
 2. What does it mean to "hate" family? _____
    _____
 3. How should a disciple react if family criticizes, ridicules, or discourages his or her new relationship with Jesus?
    _____
    _____
 4. Does "family time" (ball games, picnics, outings, etc.) come before serving Jesus? _____
 5. Jesus gives specific instructions regarding the disciple's treatment of family in Ephesians 5-6. We will examine those instructions in another lesson, but at this point you must understand that following Jesus is more important than pleasing your family.

C. The disciple obeys Jesus and does not allow possessions to control him.
 1. Many are driven by and obsessed with their material possessions such as money, cars, houses, and clothes.

LESSON 1 Disciples Prioritize   11

2. Luke gives us Jesus' perspective on material goods in Luke 12:15. Read this passage now.

    a. What is covetousness? _____

    b. Are possessions more important than following Jesus? _____

    c. Should the desire for more "stuff" destroy our ability to follow Jesus Christ? _____

3. Read Luke 18:18-23. Why didn't this man follow Jesus?_____

4. The disciple needs to be certain that possessions do not dictate how life is lived: "For what _____ is it to a man if he gains the whole world, and is himself destroyed or lost?" (Luke 9:25).

D. The disciple obeys Jesus at all times.

   1. Jesus teaches us to take up our cross "daily" (Luke 9:23).

   2. Christianity is not performed only on Sunday in a church building.

   3. The disciple continually follows Jesus, i.e., the disciple changes self to be like Jesus.

   4. At work, if an employer or superior asks a disciple to do wrong will he or she do so?_____

   5. At school, will a disciple cheat on an exam or copy someone else's homework assignment?_____

   6. At home, will each partner try to get his or her own way, so fighting and strife mar the home?_____

   7. Ultimately, discipleship becomes something we are, not something we do. It is a continual manner of life.

E. The disciple obeys Jesus despite opposition from the world.

   1. The world cannot understand disciples. They think we are missing out on all the "fun" of sin and wonder why we are not joining them (read 1 Peter 4:4).

2. However, disciples find great contentment and joy from living as Jesus commands because they know this way of life leads to heaven (John 14:1-6). Disciples understand that reaching heaven is far more important than pleasing their peers.

3. Disciples can resist peer pressure by remembering that life in the world is ultimately vain and empty because it does not lead to heaven. Abundant living and contentment can only be found in Jesus (John 10:10).

★ 4. Make up your mind now that you will never go back to the vanity of worldliness but will continue to learn more and more about being a disciple of Christ.

5. "No one, having put his hand to the plow, and looking back, is fit for the kingdom of God" (Luke 9:62). Don't look back!

III. Conclusion

A. Christianity is a way of life in which we attempt to become like Jesus.

B. In every situation and circumstance Christ's disciple asks, "What would Jesus do?," or "How would Jesus act in this situation?"

C. Obedience to Jesus determines whether we are true disciples of Christ.

D. The disciple lives in obedience to Jesus because this is the only way to receive the reward of heaven.

E. What parts of your life are not like Jesus? Use the following space to write down some specific actions and behaviors that need changing. No one will look at your list or use it to embarrass or shame you. This exercise is for your personal use only and will help you identify problem areas that need prayer, discipline, and effort. Note: this is not something only new Christians need to do. All Christians must continually evaluate themselves and their walk with God (see 2 Corinthians 13:5).

1. Home _____
   _____
   _____
   _____

2. Job _____
   _____
   _____
   _____

3. Truth and integrity _____
   _____
   _____
   _____

4. Influencing others_____
   _____
   _____
   _____

5. Resisting temptation_____
   _____
   _____
   _____

Lesson 2

Disciples Pray

A. Would you be excited if the President of the United States invited you for a personal visit at the White House?

B. Prayer is exciting because it is communication with the most powerful Being in the universe, Jehovah God! In this lesson you will learn:

1. Why you need to be taught how to pray.
2. How to pray effectively.
3. What to pray for.

C. Text: Luke 11:1-4—read this now.

I. Why do I need to be taught how to pray?

A. Prayer is a learned activity.
1. Prayer does not necessarily "flow" spontaneously or naturally.
2. Jesus' disciples had prayed many times but saw in Jesus a prayer life they simply had to know more about.
3. They asked Jesus to teach them to pray. We need to do the same.

B. There is a great deal of false information about prayer.
1. Some teach that prayer is only a mental boost for the one praying. They say this because they don't believe in God or that He will respond to His creation. Prayer is then just a psychological crutch.
2. Others teach that prayer is like magic and needs to be chanted or done while holding special religious charms.
3. Many turn prayer into a "gimme" session. They seem to believe prayer makes God into some sort of cosmic vending machine, forcing Him to dispense whatever we desire.

4. With all of these erroneous ideas about prayer we need to be taught the truth about prayer by Jesus.

C. We need to learn to be like our Teacher.

1. Disciples want to be like their teacher—Luke 6:40.

2. Read in Luke: 3:21; 5:16; 6:12; 9:18, 29; 22:41-44.

3. Did Jesus make time for prayer? _____

4. Are you ready to be like Jesus, praying often and fervently?
_____

II. What did Jesus teach about praying?

A. Prayer is simple.

1. The Lord's prayer is simple and direct.

2. Notice that Jesus does not pray with high-sounding religious language or flowery cliches.

3. The disciple should pray as Jesus prayed: simply and directly.

4. Do not feel obligated to add Shakespeare's English to your prayers. "Thee" and "thou" do not make prayer more acceptable, and since we do not use this language today, may hinder authentic prayer. Such language is not wrong, but it is not necessary.

B. Prayer is the basis of our relationship with God.

1. How does Jesus address God? _____
_____

2. Can we call God "Father?" _____

3. On what basis does the Christian call God "Father" (read Romans 8:15 and Galatians 4:6)? _____
_____

4. Read Luke 11:5-13. What concept of God does Jesus want His disciples to have when Jesus calls God, "Father"?_____
_____

C. Christ's prayer is about God's will, not ours.

LESSON 2 Disciples Pray   17

1. Analyze Jesus' prayer in Luke 11:1-4. Does Jesus pray about His personal needs or about doing the will of God? _____
   _____

2. Read Luke 22:41-42. What is the crux of Jesus' prayer here?
   _____
   _____

★ 3. Many think prayer ought to change our circumstances (and it can), but Jesus' prayer shows us that prayer can do more than change external situations. Prayer changes us! In prayer we learn to seek God's will and are strengthened to do His will.

III. **For what did Jesus teach us to pray?**

   A. "Hallowed be Your Name"

   1. Hallowing is an act of setting something apart for sacred purposes.

   2. The first part of Jesus' prayer expresses a desire for the Person of God (as represented by His name) to be set apart as unique and separate (see Ezekiel 36:23).

   3. To pray this is to recognize God's greatness, majesty and power, and how small and weak we truly are.

   B. "Your kingdom come"

   1. The term "kingdom" often refers to the church which is the body of saved people (Mark 9:1; Colossians 1:13). In this sense, the kingdom has come and is already present.

   2. The Bible also uses "kingdom" to refer to God's rule and reign in people's hearts: "For indeed, the _____ of God is within you" (Luke 17:21).

   3. In this sense, the kingdom is always coming, as men and women submit their lives to Christ. Thus, praying for the kingdom to come can be seen as a request for God to work in our lives, to rule and reign in our hearts.

   4. Submitting to God and allowing the kingdom to come in our own lives and hearts is of supreme importance and worthy of our efforts in prayer.

5. Further, this is a prayer for evangelism. Jesus prays that more people will be taught about Him and respond to Him by becoming disciples. Disciples also must pray for evangelism opportunities.

C. "Daily bread"

1. This is a prayer for daily necessities and shows how the disciple recognizes his or her total dependence upon God. Even the smallest of life's daily provisions comes from God!

★ 2. Notice that Jesus says nothing about praying for luxuries that fall in the category of wants rather than needs.

3. How much bread does Jesus ask for? _____

4. This kind of prayer cultivates trust in God, as He supplies our needs day by day.

D. "Forgive us our sins"

1. This is one of the most crucial parts of prayer. What does sin do to one's relationship with God (see Isaiah 59:1-2)?
   _____

2. How is the Christian to secure forgiveness of sin (see Acts 8:20-23; 1 John 1:8-9)? _____
   _____

3. Despite our best efforts we will do wrong. Without the opportunity to pray and seek forgiveness we would have no chance of heaven. Do you see how important prayer is?
   _____

E. "Do not lead us...deliver us from the evil one."

1. Forgiveness is not enough. Jesus prayed for protection from sin.

2. Read 1 Corinthians 10:13. Will God help you escape temptation? _____

3. Read James 4:7. Can we resist the devil successfully? _____

4. This part of the Lord's prayer asks God to assist His children in escaping sin. Do you need to pray this prayer? _____

IV. Conclusion

A. We would be excited to meet a movie star, statesman or famous person.

   1. Now you understand that prayer is more important, more powerful, and more meaningful than any meeting with a person, no matter how famous they are or how much power they claim.

   2. No one cares for us as God does, and no one can do the things that He can do. Prayer is our communication with our great God.

B. It is important that you begin doing what you have learned.

   1. Study the Lord's Prayer. Use it as a model upon which to build your prayer life.

   2. Obviously, this prayer is not designed to be exclusive and prohibit any other requests or needs. There is nothing that cannot be taken before God (see Philippians 4:6).

   3. Prayer is designed to be a tremendous blessing. Pray as Jesus did and you will discover this is true.

   4. Plan to pray regularly. God wants to hear from you!

20 Who Will Follow Jesus?

LESSON 3 Disciples Work Together

Lesson 3

Disciples Work Together

A. Is being a disciple a solo venture? What is the disciple's relationship to other followers of Jesus?

B. Luke 6:12-16 records the call of the apostles. Read this text now.

1. Significantly, Jesus did not call only one apostle.

2. Instead, a group was assembled. They worked together as Jesus' ambassadors to spread the gospel into all the world.

3. Luke's account of these followers continues in his sequel work, Acts. This book shows the apostles as the beginning and foundation of the church, the saved actively following Jesus.

4. Jesus did not mean for disciples to function alone. Disciples come together in a special group arrangement known as the church.

C. In this lesson you will learn:

1. What the local church means to the disciple.

2. Why a disciple should join a local church.

3. What obligations and responsibilities disciples have to the local church.

I. What is the local church?

A. The New Testament uses the term "church" in two different ways:

1. It designates all saved people: "To the general assembly and _____ of the firstborn who are registered in heaven" (Hebrews 12:23).

2. It designates a group of disciples in a certain city or community: "To the church of God which is at _____" (1 Corinthians 1:2).

3. When referring to all the saved, we are speaking of the universal church. The universal church is composed of everyone who is a Christian, living or dead. Some members of the universal church are on earth, and some are in heaven.
    a. In the universal sense there is only one church (Ephesians 4:4).
    b. There exists no earthly organization or headquarters for the universal church. Jesus Christ is its Head (Ephesians 1:22-23).
4. If one is speaking of a certain group of Christians, one may speak of the local church. This is the band of disciples in a certain place. In the local sense there are many congregations.
5. Neither "universal church" nor "local church" are terms found specifically in the Bible, but they express scriptural concepts. Do you understand the difference in these terms?_____

B. Can you join the church?

★ 1. No one can join the universal church because its membership is not controlled by humans.
2. Read Acts 2:47. Who adds people to the universal church?
   _____
3. What is the entrance requirement for the universal church?
   _____
4. While we cannot join the universal church, but must be added to it by God, it is possible to attach oneself to a local body of Christians.
5. Read what Luke wrote about Saul in Acts 9:26-28. What did Saul want to do ? _____
   We too must join a local church.

C. What does it mean to place membership (join) a local church?
1. Joining a local congregation is a serious commitment because the local church has important work to accomplish.
2. Every member is needed to carry out the local church's threefold mission:

a. Preach the gospel to the lost: Matthew 28:19-20.

b. Build up Christians spiritually: Ephesians 4:11-16.

c. Relieve needy Christians: 1 Timothy 5:16.

3. When a disciple joins a local church he or she is announcing the intention to help that congregation fulfill the assignments for the local church.

II. **Why should a disciple join a local church?**

A. The local church promotes accountability.

1. Sometimes, following Jesus is difficult. Disciples can be tempted to abandon Christianity.

2. Yet, we know that if we quit the Lord, other disciples will ask about our conduct and actions. This helps us remain faithful.

3. Read Galatians 6:1. Should brethren assist each other?
   _____

4. Accountability and restoration are two key functions of elders. Read Hebrews 13:17. Should we respect the elders?
   _____

5. No one has the right to pry into private matters just to satisfy personal curiosity. However, Christians should expect the family of God to assist them in growing stronger by holding them accountable for their actions.

B. The local church provides instruction.

1. The local church's main focus is teaching the lost the gospel, and teaching Christians how to be better disciples (1 Timothy 3:15).

2. Every Christian should expect the local congregation to provide instruction in discipleship.

3. The basis for such instruction must be the Scriptures. Read Luke 24:27. What did Jesus explain in His teaching?
   _____
   _____
   _____

4. Good Bible study is not made up of sharing opinions or reading books written by human authors. Instead, the local church teaches the Bible, showing how the Scriptures relate to Jesus and His will for disciples.

C. The local church is where the disciple can develop his or her talents.

1. Disciples do not all have the same ability, but every disciple has some talent that can be used in the Kingdom of God.
2. "For as we have many members in one body, but all the members do not have the same function, so we, being many, are one body in Christ, and individually members of one another" (Romans 12:4-5).
3. Some can teach Bible classes, others can do physical work around the meeting place, while still others visit the sick and elderly. The list of activities needed in a local church never ends!
4. Find someone at the local church who is already doing what you might be able to do. Ask them to help you learn how to put your talent to use for the Lord.

★ 5. Every talent, no matter how small it may seem to others, is needed in the Body of Christ.

6. Read 1 Corinthians 12:20-21. Are you needed in the church?

III. What obligations and responsibilities do disciples have to the local church?

A. Disciples accept responsibility.

1. Read Luke 10:1-3. Jesus charged these disciples with certain tasks.
2. Christianity is not a "free ride" in which everyone constantly caters to your every need.
3. It is vital that you understand the duties, obligations, and responsibilities that God has given you to fulfill in the local church.

LESSON 3 Disciples Work Together 25

- B. Disciples help keep the local church united.
    1. Unity among disciples is extremely important to Jesus.
    2. Read John 17:20-21. Should Jesus' disciples be divided?_____
    3. Fussing, fighting, and dividing are strongly condemned throughout the New Testament (see 1 Corinthians 1:10-13; Ephesians 4:31).
    4. Unity cannot be maintained at the expense of truth (Galatians 1:8-9), but division over anything but truth is inexcusable.
    5. You can assist the local church in building and maintaining unity by refusing to gossip (1 Timothy 5:13, 19), by not taking part in arguments over inconsequential matters (2 Timothy 2:23), and by being a peacemaker to brethren with problems (Matthew 5:9).
- C. Disciples attend worship services faithfully.
    1. We are commanded to "not _____ the assembling of ourselves together, as is the manner of some" (Hebrews 10:25).
    2. Perhaps nothing else will make or break your spiritual vitality as much as your attitude toward attendance. Those who fail to attend fail at Christianity. This means they will be lost.
    3. Regular attendance provides the Christian with the opportunity to examine his or her life and rededicate self to the Lord, recharge spiritually, and serve others.
    ★ 4. Attending regularly begins with deciding to be at every service possible, a complete refusal to excuse or rationalize failure to attend, and a determination to schedule everything else around service times. Faithful attendance is a habit: once it is started, it is easy to maintain. Begin building this habit now!
- D. Disciples worship sincerely and genuinely.
    1. We must "worship in spirit and truth." (John 4:24).
    2. True worship means we have the right attitude (the heart or spirit) and the right actions (as set forth by God's truth, the Bible).

3. The right attitude demands that we worship with an awareness that God is watching our worship and every action must please Him.

   a. Reverence, a deep respect for God, controls us as we worship.

   b. It is not possible for one to be self-centered, or flippant in mind and heart while worshipping God (see Psalms 89:7).

4. Worship includes singing. Read Ephesians 5:19. What is important in singing: musical ability or thinking about the words sung? _____

5. Prayer is part of worship—Acts 2:42.

6. Giving counts! Study 1 Corinthians 16:1-2; 2 Corinthians 8:9.

   a. Does God set a certain percentage that disciples must give? _____

   b. Proper giving involves planning, generosity, and a glad heart.

7. Teaching or preaching is part of worship—read 2 Timothy 4:2. What should preaching do? _____
   _____

8. The Lord's Supper is essential—read 1 Corinthians 11:23-29.

   a. What does the disciple do during the Lord's Supper?
   _____
   _____

   b. What is the purpose of the Lord's Supper? _____
   _____

★ 9. Worship is a verb. It is an action word. Make certain you are actively taking part in the worship services by involving your mind and body in worship that pleases God.

E. Disciples live a life that reflects well on the local church.

   1. Christians are a living advertisement for (or against) Christianity.

LESSON 3 Disciples Work Together

2. "Walk in _____ toward those who are outside" (Colossians 4:5).

3. Some unbelievers delight in seeing Christians who are living sinfully. Are such Christians truly following Jesus? _____

4. The disciple wants to set a positive example before unbelievers so that opportunities to teach the lost will be created (1 Peter 2:12).

IV. **Conclusion**

A. Discipleship is not a solo task. The disciple needs other disciples.

1. While one cannot join the universal church, it is important that every disciple become part of a local church.

2. The local church provides excellent opportunities for service, growth, and faithfulness.

3. With the blessings of the local church also come great responsibilities. The disciple must accept these obligations as part of following Jesus.

B. Young Christians are so vulnerable to the devil's tricks and temptations.

1. Do not isolate yourself from other Christians. Doing so invites spiritual disaster.

2. Become part of a local congregation of the Lord's people.

3. Being a working part of a local church is essential to being an effective disciple.

Lesson 4

Disciples Think and Ask Questions

A. How does the disciple grow to be more like Jesus? How does the disciple know what God wants him to do?

B. As a newborn Christian it is essential that you regularly study God's word so that you can grow in Jesus Christ (read 1 Peter 2:2).

C. In this lesson you will learn:
   1. Why asking questions is so important.
   2. How to find God's will in the Bible.
   3. Techniques for studying the Bible effectively and profitably.

I. **Parables and questions**

   A. Read Luke 8:4-15.
      1. A parable is an earthly story with a heavenly meaning.
      2. Identify the earthly story: _____
         _____
      3. Can you find the heavenly meaning? _____
         _____
      4. Did everyone understand the parable? _____
         Why not? _____
         _____
      5. Some who didn't understand did something very important that enabled them to understand (v. 9). What did they do?
         _____

   B. Key principle: Disciples think and ask questions.
      1. The disciples were not content to merely hear a story about farming. They pressed for more.
      2. Disciples today must do the same. We cannot be content to let someone tell us what the Bible teaches or what we should believe.

3. Creeds, edicts, and dogmas from denominational councils are all attempts to replace the process of Bible study with human ideas.
4. Some religious groups do not want their members to search the Scriptures for themselves or to ask questions about the various events, activities, procedures, and teachings that are being implemented. Is this consistent with the spirit of Christ and discipleship? _____

C. What kind of questions do disciples ask?
1. The primary question must always be "What does the Bible say?"
2. What people think, write, or say is not as important as Scripture. Disciples must ask "Does this teaching match the Bible's teaching?"
3. Hear Paul's strong warning: "But even if we, or an _____ from heaven, preach any other _____ to you than what we have preached to you, let him be accursed. As we have said before, so now I say again, if anyone preaches any other _____ to you than what you have received, let him be accursed" (Galatians 1:8-9).
4. If someone claims a teaching is from God, do disciples automatically assume it is so? _____
5. Is it wrong to ask questions or inquire about someone's teachings (see 1 John 4:1; Revelation 2:2)? _____
6. Jesus' disciples must not accept any teaching without first checking it against Scripture to see if it is true.
7. "These [in the city of Berea] were more fair-minded than those in Thessalonica, in that they _____ the word with all readiness, and _____ the _____ daily to find out whether these things were so" (Acts 17:11).
8. Disciples know they can trust the Bible because it is from God (2 Timothy 3:16-17). When we have God's word, we need nothing else.
9. The New Testament functions as our only pattern and guide today. We must do exactly as it says, no more and no less (Galatians 1:8-9).

LESSON 4 Disciples Think and Ask Questions   31

    10. Knowing the Scriptures is the key to discerning truth from error. Are you ready to study the Bible to understand God's will? _____

II. How do we find God's will in the scriptures?

    A. Rightly divide the Word of God.

        1. Confusing the Old and New Testaments causes error.

        2. Read Galatians 3:24-25. What function did the Law of Moses serve? _____

        3. Now that "faith" has come, are we still under the tutor? _____

        4. What law are Christians under now? (see Galatians 6:2) _____

    B. Obey direct commands.

        1. Much of God's will for us is communicated in plain, simple terms.

        2. Peter's preaching contained clear commands: "Repent, and let every one of you be baptized..." (Acts 2:38).

        3. Jesus' desires regarding His Supper are not hard to understand: "This do...in remembrance of Me" (1 Corinthians 11:25).

        4. Giving is clearly specified: "On the first day of the week let each one of you lay something aside..." (1 Corinthians 16:2).

    C. Observe approved examples.

        1. Approved examples are simply the practices of the New Testament church as it functioned under the guidance of the apostles.

        2. The New Testament urges us to follow the example of the apostles: "The things which you _____ and received and heard and saw in me, these do, and the _____ of peace will be with you" (Philippians 4:9).

        3. "Stand fast and hold the _____ which you were taught, whether by word or our epistle" (2 Thessalonians 2:15).

4. Human tradition is not important, but apostolic tradition is from God and must be followed.

5. Watching the example of the apostles and New Testament church helps us know many things:

    a. Acts 20:7—when did the church take the Lord's Supper?
    _____

    b. Acts 14:23—did the apostles teach one man should rule the church or several men should serve as elders?
    _____

D. Draw forced conclusions.

1. God expects disciples to reason to logical conclusions. The Bible presents the facts. We draw the conclusion the text forces us to draw.

2. Read Matthew 3:16. The Bible nowhere says Jesus went down into the water, but if He came up from the water, sound reasoning concludes that He went down into it.

3. Exodus 20:8 instructed Israel to keep the Sabbath holy. Since no other instruction is given, the only conclusion possible was that God wanted Israel to hallow every Sabbath.

4. Acts 20:7 tells us disciples took the Lord's Supper on Sunday. 1 Corinthians 16:1-2 shows us disciples met for worship every Sunday. Regarding the frequency of taking the Lord's Supper what conclusion does the New Testament force us to draw?

    ❑ We should take the Supper once a year.

    ❑ We should take the Supper every Sunday, just as the New Testament church did.

E. Summary:

1. Following Christ means we obey Him. The disciple constantly searches to find Bible authority for every activity and doctrine.

2. Disciples ask, "What passage commands this?," "Where is the example?," or "How did we draw this conclusion?"

LESSON 4 Disciples Think and Ask Questions   33

   3. In these ways God's will is communicated to us, and we must obey it.

★ 4. If a teaching or practice cannot be established by command, example, or conclusion, we know that it is not God's will.

   5. "And whatever you do in word or deed, do all in the name of the Lord Jesus…" (Colossians 3:17).

III. **Bible Study Keys**

   A. Bible study key 1: regular study

      1. Few things are meaningful if practiced haphazardly.

      2. Read your Bible daily to reap the greatest benefits from it.

      3. Study 2 Timothy 2:15. What does "give diligence" mean?
         _____

   B. Bible study key 2: don't study over your head

      1. Some parts of the Bible are more difficult than others.

      2. "But solid _____ belongs to those who are of full age, that is, those who by reason of use have their _____ exercised to discern both good and evil" (Hebrews 5:14).

      3. Try reading Luke or Mark. Jesus' teachings are easy to understand and extraordinarily practical. These books will be of immediate help to you.

      4. Next read Acts which contains the account of what the first disciples did after Jesus left earth and returned to heaven.

      5. Wait to tackle the more difficult material such as Revelation or Daniel until you have a better feel for the overall message and theme of the Bible.

   C. Bible study key 3: turn reading into Bible study

      1. Don't settle for mere reading. Study the Bible by asking three questions as you read. This will maximize your time in the word.

      2. What is going on in this text?

a. Be sure you understand the who, what, and where of the reading. Who are the main characters? What are they doing? Where are they?
   b. A Bible encyclopedia, atlas, or dictionary can help you with these questions. These are available in the church's library, from a bookstore, or may be borrowed from another Christian.
3. Why is this in the Bible?
   a. Why did God choose to record this information?
   b. How does it fit into the Bible's theme, the salvation of man from sin?
   c. What does the text teach us about God, man, sin, and righteousness?
4. How can I apply this to my life?
   a. Don't let Bible study be just facts and interesting trivia.
   b. Always examine your life in the light of His word and see where corrections or improvements need to be made.
★ 5. Extra tip: consider keeping a notebook in which you may write down the results of your study. We remember much more of what we studied when we take notes.

IV. Conclusion

A. Disciples are seekers of truth.
   1. Because of this, disciples are never afraid to ask "Why are we doing this?" or "How do we know it is God's will to teach this?"
   2. Disciples want to know the truth! True disciples are completely unwilling to accept anything but Bible truth as an answer.
   3. Our questions about discipleship must drive us to the Bible for answers.
B. We can know God's truth through the Bible.
   1. That truth can be communicated through direct commands.

LESSON 4 Disciples Think and Ask Questions

    2. God wants us to observe the New Testament Christians in action and learn truth from their example.

    3. Often, the Bible forces us to an obvious conclusion about God's will.

    4. Disciples use all three of these methods to discern truth.

C. You can read and understand your Bible.

    1. Read regularly.

    2. Read material you can understand.

    3. Do more than read—study the Bible.

D. Disciples who do these things will be able to walk with God in confidence that they are obeying the truth.

36 Who Will Follow Jesus?

Disciples Love Others

   A. As a disciple how do I treat others? What do I do when people treat me badly? What is my attitude toward others?

   B. Being a follower of Christ radically changes your relationships with others. In this lesson you will learn:

      1. What it means to love others.

      2. Specific applications of the principle of love.

   C. Text: Luke 6:27-38—read this now.

I. What does it mean to love others?

   A. Today, many are confused by the term "love."

      1. Many different concepts are implied by the word "love."

      2. People readily acknowledge that they love their country, pets, favorite foods, favorite sports team, and family.

      3. There are different kinds of love, even though we use one term to describe all of them.

      4. In the New Testament, originally written in Greek, there are different words for love. Each term expresses a unique relationship.

   B. What does Jesus mean when He says, "Love your enemies" (Luke 6:27)?

      1. Jesus is not speaking of erotic, sensual love (Greek: *eros*).

      2. This is not brotherly, "good friend" love (Greek: *phileo*). Phileo love is what we feel for people we find likable and who like us.

      3. Jesus uses the Greek term *agape*. This term came to mean a special love that puts the best interests of others ahead of our own desires and wants.

38 Who Will Follow Jesus?

   ★ 4. This is not a feeling but a conscious act of will. The disciple constantly seeks other's good.

   5. Read Romans 5:8. Have God and Jesus shown us *agape* love? _____

   6. If we are to be like Christ, what kind of love must we have for others, even if they are our enemies? _____

II. **How does *agape* love act?**

   A. *Agape* love refuses to seek personal revenge.

   1. Read Luke 6:27-29 again. List the wrongs Jesus says the disciple endures without striking back: _____ _____

   2. Study Romans 12:17-21: "Do not _____ anyone evil for evil...Beloved, never _____ yourselves, but leave room for the wrath of God; for it is written, Vengeance is mine, I will repay, says the Lord...Do not be _____ by evil, but overcome evil with good."

   3. Can the disciple take revenge? _____
      Whose job is vengeance? _____

   4. How do disciples overcome evil? _____ _____

   B. *Agape* love helps the needy, even if they cannot repay it.

   1. "But _____ your enemies, do good, and lend, hoping for _____ in return; and your _____ will be great, and you will be sons of the Most High" (Luke 6:35).

   2. Read Jesus' story on helping the helpless in Luke 10:30-37.

   3. List some of the specific ways the Good Samaritan helped the wounded man: _____ _____

   4. Did the Good Samaritan help only those who could repay him? _____

   5. Did the Good Samaritan show *agape* love to the robbery victim? _____

LESSON 5 Disciples Love Others 39

C. *Agape* love refuses to be judgmental.

1. "Judge not, and you shall not be _____. Condemn not, and you shall not be _____. Forgive, and you will be _____" (Luke 6:37).

2. Some people are always condemning others. This was the attitude of the Pharisees, who even condemned Jesus for healing people on the Sabbath (Luke 6:6-11). This only shows hard-heartedness.

3. Disciples accept and care for others. They realize that each one of us is a sinner who needs God's help (Romans 3:23).

4. Does this mean that disciples cannot tell someone that they are lost or that they are transgressing God's law? _____

   a. What does John 7:24 tell us about this? _____
   _____

   b. Read Matthew 7:1-5. What kind of judging is Jesus forbidding (note verse 5)? _____
   _____

III. Who needs *agape* love?

A. Enemies need *agape* love.

1. When we stand for righteousness, some will oppose us.

2. "This is the condemnation, that the _____ has come into the world, and men loved _____ rather than light, because their deeds were evil. For everyone practicing _____ hates the light and does not come to the light, lest his _____ should be exposed" (John 3:19-20).

★ 3. We must still seek our enemies' best interest by trying to bring them to Jesus Christ.

4. Praying for those who oppose us may be the greatest expression of loving enemies.

B. Our homes need *agape* love.

1. If we treat our enemies with *agape* love, we should definitely treat our family with the same consideration and love.

2. Read Ephesians 5:22-29.

   a. How can a wife show love for her husband? _____
   _____

   b. After whom do husbands model love for their wives?
   _____

   c. Would any marriage fail if both partners committed themselves to *agape* love? _____

C. The church needs *agape* love.

   1. The New Testament clearly instructs disciples to love and care for one another.

   2. If a brother or sister is in need: "But whoever has this world's goods, and sees his _____ in need, and shuts up his heart from him, how does the _____ of God abide in him? My little children, let us not _____ in word or in tongue, but in deed and in truth" (1 John 3:17-18).

   3. If a brother or sister is caught up in sin: "Brethren, if a man is _____ in any trespass, you who are spiritual _____ such a one in a spirit of gentleness, considering yourself lest you also be tempted. _____ one another's burdens, and so fulfill the law of Christ" (Galatians 6:1-2).

   4. When we disagree or have been wronged by another Christian: "Therefore, as the elect of God, holy and beloved, put on tender mercies, _____, humility, meekness, longsuffering, bearing with one another, and _____ one another, if anyone has a _____ against another; even as Christ forgave you, so you also must do. But above all these things put on _____ which is the bond of perfection" (Colossians 3:12-14).

   5. God hates contention among brethren (Proverbs 6:19). Satan rejoices when brethren refuse to get along and help each other because it destroys the church's ability to proclaim the gospel (John 13:33-34).

   6. Would any church ever suffer inner strife and division if every brother and sister in Christ determined to love with *agape* love?

IV. **Conclusion**
   A. Being a disciple of Christ changes how we treat everyone.
      1. In every relationship the disciple of Christ practices *agape* love.
      2. This means disciples seek what is best for others.
      3. *Agape* love is the love that Jesus demonstrated for us (1 John 4:19) and must be part of our lives if we are going to be like Him.
   B. Every relationship can benefit from *agape* love.
      1. From enemies, to the home, to the church we find people needing sincere, genuine love.
      2. As the disciple models Christ's love in every place and situation, others can see the difference being a Christian makes.
      3. "Let your light so shine before men, that they may see your good works and glorify your Father in heaven" (Matthew 5:16).

Lesson 6

Disciples Teach Others

A. How should disciples help others come to know Jesus Christ? Can you be an effective teacher of the gospel?

B. Jesus wants all of His disciples to be teaching others about Him: "Go and make disciples of all the nations, baptizing them in the name of the Father and of the Son and of the Holy Spirit, teaching them to observe all things that I have commanded you" (Matthew 28:19-20).

C. In this lesson you will learn:

1. How to prepare yourself to teach others.

2. What the disciple should teach.

3. Keys to effective teaching.

I. Getting ready to teach

A. Recognize the responsibility of teaching.

1. The teacher must be sure to never lead students away from truth.

2. To drive people away from Christ Jesus with our tactics or techniques is clearly a mistake.

3. Teaching the Bible is a serious task—it influences the eternal destiny of souls (James 3:1)!

B. Pray

1. Prayer is the beginning of all gospel teaching ventures.

2. Hear Jesus: "The _____ truly is great, but the laborers are few; therefore _____ the Lord of the harvest to send out _____ into His harvest" (Luke 10:2).

3. The New Testament church was continually involved in prayer. Note what they prayed for:

a. Acts 4:24-31 _____
_____

b. Acts 13:2-3 _____
_____

★ 4. Without God's blessings upon us we are sure to fail miserably. We must pray if we are going to succeed.

5. In the context of evangelism, for what should we pray?

   a. Pray for opportunities to teach.

   b. Pray that the ones you teach will be receptive.

   c. Pray that you will have wisdom while teaching.

C. Assemble your knowledge.

1. Every disciple needs to be ready to justify and defend Christianity.

2. "But sanctify the Lord God in your _____, and always be ready to give a _____ to everyone who asks you a _____ for the hope that is in you, with meekness and fear" (1 Peter 3:15).

3. We need to know why we believe what we believe and be ready to explain this to any one who asks.

4. This involves knowing:

   a. Why we believe in God.

   b. Why we believe the Bible is His word.

   c. What God has done so we may be saved.

   d. How we respond to God's grace so that we may be saved.

5. You already have a head start on these concepts because these are the very things you have just learned and done to become a Christian.

6. Consider memorizing key passages of scripture that you will need in teaching others (such as Acts 2:38; 22:16; Galatians 1:8-9).

7. Many books, videos, and other aids can help you strengthen your ability to communicate soul-saving truths. If you need

help, ask the one who taught you the gospel or is teaching this lesson, or the elders or preacher at the congregation where you are a member.

II. What to teach

A. Focus on Christ Jesus.

1. The disciple's message is based on the fact that Christ Jesus came to earth, died for everyone's sins, arose from the dead, and will return one day to judge the world (1 Corinthians 15:1-5).

2. This is the apostolic message which has been preached from Pentecost until now: "Because He has appointed a _____ on which He will judge the world in _____ by the Man whom He has ordained…" (Acts 17:31).

3. We must be certain that we are not preaching ourselves or our own ideas but that we are preaching Jesus Christ.

B. Focus on the authority of the Bible.

1. For too many people the Bible is only a "good book," which is full of old stories and interesting people, but it is not seen as the authoritative word of God.

2. Many do not understand that they cannot add to or take away from the Bible (Galatians 1:8-9). Others do not understand the difference between the Old and New Testaments (Galatians 3:23-24).

3. Many do not accept the Bible as being God's instruction book which they must obey.

4. In order to help others respond to Jesus, we must help them see that the Bible is not just a good book. It is God's book which contains God's will for their lives.

5. "He who _____ Me, and does not receive My words, has that which _____ him; the word that I have spoken will judge him in the last day" (John 12:48).

★ 6. Until a person accepts the Bible as the absolute standard in his or her life, it is useless to discuss anything else.

7. So, we must ask people, "What do you think of the Bible?" and work to bring them to the point where they have genuine faith in God's word.

C. Do not quibble or quarrel.

1. "And a servant of the Lord must not _____ but be gentle to all, able to _____, patient in humility correcting those who are in opposition" (2 Timothy 2:24-25).

2. Some people just want to "play games," argue, and squabble about religion.

3. They have no intention of changing, placing trust in Jesus Christ, or seeking truth. They just enjoy a good fuss.

4. Disciples need to be careful not to be drawn into fruitless, endless controversy.

5. Jesus refused to quibble with people. Read Luke 20:1-8.

    a. What question did the Pharisees ask Jesus?_____
    _____

    b. What question did Jesus ask them? _____
    _____

    c. Why wouldn't Jesus answer their question? _____
    _____

6. Arguing about how many angels can dance on the head of a pin, did Adam have a belly button, etc. is vain and useless. Don't waste your time on such nonsense (2 Timothy 2:16).

III. Keys to effective teaching

A. Be patient.

1. Some will not see the truth as quickly as others.

2. Many preconceived notions and prejudices must be overcome.

3. Let people learn at their own pace, not yours!

4. Jesus was long-suffering with people (see John 4:6-26). We must be like Christ and be patient.

LESSON 6 Disciples Teach Others 47

- B. Listen.
    1. In the Gospel of Luke we see Jesus continually asking people questions and then listening carefully to their response (Luke 9:20).
    2. Jesus knew that He could find out where people were in their development and knowledge by asking questions.
    3. We need to do the same—listen, listen, listen.
- C. Be a friend.
    1. People are very suspicious of "hard sell" types who appear to be trying to "pawn off" some slick product.
    2. Be like Jesus—concerned about other people in a genuine, caring way. How did Jesus show He cared in the following scriptures?
        - a. Luke 5:13 _____
        - b. Luke 7:11-16 _____
        - c. Luke 8:41-48 _____
        - d. Luke 18:15-17 _____
    ★ 3. Because there is much false religion and teaching in our world, many times you must earn a hearing for the gospel message by showing how it works in your own life.
    4. "Let your _____ so shine before men, that they may see your good _____ and glorify your _____ in heaven" (Matthew 5:16).
- D. Do the work of evangelism.
    1. We can only prepare and plan so long. Eventually we must be about the business of teaching the lost.
    2. Commit a definite amount of time to evangelism every week.
    3. Look for contacts by greeting every non-Christian visitor at the worship services, getting acquainted with your neighbors and co-workers, or by inviting someone to a regular service of the church.

★ 4. Other ideas: Distribute DVDs or CDs of Bible teaching, hand out tracts, use social media to post about the Bible and church, have a stronger Christian teach a small-group Bible study in your home, or message, email or phone acquaintances to ask them to read the Bible with you.

5. There are many ways we can be involved in evangelism. Work a method that you are comfortable with—but be sure to work!

IV. Conclusion

A. All disciples need to be teaching others about Jesus Christ.

1. Prepare yourself so you can be an effective teacher of the gospel.

2. Always watch for opportunities to teach people about Jesus.

3. While you may not feel extremely confident now, you can still learn more, and you can still tell others what you did to become a Christian and why you did those things.

B. Some become discouraged when teaching, but they should not.

1. Yes, it is disappointing that not everyone will do what the Bible says and become a Christian.

2. However, Jesus has not charged us with converting people but teaching people. Read the Great Commission text (Matthew 28:19-20) and note the priority of teaching.

3. We teach. The prospect then decides what to do with the information we give him or her (read 1 Corinthians 3:5-9).

4. Do not put too much pressure on yourself. You please God when you try—and anyone can try!

C. List five people you want to talk with about the gospel. Begin praying for these people and looking for an opportunity to discuss Jesus with them.

1. _____

2. _____

3. _____

4. _____

5. _____

Lesson 7

Disciples Fail but Never Quit

A. What do I do when I sin? Do I need to be baptized again after I sin? What does Jesus think of me when I fail Him?

B. New disciples quickly realize that they have not mastered sin. No matter how hard they try, disciples find that they will, in some areas, do wrong. In this lesson you will learn:

1. That disciples will fail.
2. Why disciples fail.
3. What disciples do when they fail.

I. Do disciples fail?

A. Jesus' disciples failed Him often:

1. Read Luke 8:9. Did the disciples understand the parable?
   _____

2. Read Luke 8:24. Did the disciples trust Jesus as they should have? _____

3. Read Luke 9:40. Could the disciples cast out the demon?
   _____

4. Read Luke 9:46. What were the disciples arguing about?
   _____
   Should disciples argue this way? _____

5. Read Luke 22:46. Did the disciples help Jesus prepare for the suffering of the cross? _____

B. Yes, the disciples failed often.

1. But did they give up? Did the disciples get mad and quit? Did the disciples decide to start following some other teacher?

2. No, they continued to do the best they could. They kept following Jesus, and they kept trying to do better.

3. Notice the example of Peter. Read Luke 22:55-62.
    a. How many times did Peter deny Jesus? _____
    b. Was Peter sorry he did this? _____
    c. Read Luke 24:12. Did Peter give up on following Jesus?
       _____

C. Disciples do not quit.
  1. They turn back to Jesus and start following Him again.
  2. Endurance is an important part of discipleship: "Therefore we also, since we are surrounded by so great a cloud of witnesses, let us lay aside every _____, and the _____ which so easily ensnares us, and let us run with _____ the race that is set before us" (Hebrews 12:1).
  3. First-century Christians who were being terribly persecuted were told: "Be _____ until death, and I will give you the crown of _____" (Revelation 2:10).

II. Why do disciples sin?

A. Because we need to grow in Christ Jesus.
  1. When you first are born into Christ, you do not know everything about righteousness or sin.
  2. The New Testament refers to the new convert as a "babe" and points out how he or she must grow: "For everyone who partakes only of milk is unskilled in the word of righteousness, for he is a _____. But solid food belongs to those who are of full age, that is, those who by reason of use have their _____ exercised to discern both good and evil. Therefore, leaving the discussion of the _____ principles of Christ, let us go on to perfection, not laying again the foundation of _____ from dead works and of faith toward God" (Hebrews 5:13-6:1).
  3. We cannot continue in the "elementary principles of Christ" but must grow stronger and more mature in Jesus Christ.

LESSON 7 Disciples Fail but Never Quit

4. As you continue following Jesus and resisting the devil, you will get better and better at being a disciple. This is the growth and maturity process.

B. Because the devil continually tempts us.

1. The devil tempted Jesus. Read Luke 4:1-13.

    a. What was the first temptation? _____

    b. What was the second temptation? _____

    c. What was the third temptation? _____

    d. When the devil had tempted Jesus these three times, did he leave Jesus alone (note verse 13)? _____

2. Why did Judas Iscariot betray our Lord (Luke 22:3)? _____

3. Why do people sin today (James 1:13-15)? _____

4. Who is our adversary (1 Peter 5:8)? _____

5. Important: Can we resist the devil, or is falling to his temptations inevitable (James 4:7)? _____

C. Because we do not always correctly discern good and evil.

1. Some actions and thoughts are clearly shown in Scripture as wrong and forbidden to the Christian.

2. Read Galatians 5:19-21. These sins, known as the works of the flesh, represent broad categories of wrongdoing. Study this list carefully. While it does not cover every possible kind of sin, it does detail many common sins.

3. When we fail to heed the Scripture's warnings and fail to use scriptural principles to discover righteousness and evil, we will sin.

4. Discerning good and evil is a skill we acquire through diligent practice: "But solid food belongs to those who are of full age, that is, those who by reason of use have their senses _____ to discern both good and evil" (Hebrews 5:14).

★ 5. A help in discerning good from evil is to ask questions such as, "Would Jesus do this?," "What will others think if they see me doing this?," and "Will this lead to further temptation and sin?"

    a. What question did the Pharisees ask Jesus?_____

    b. What question did Jesus ask them? _____

    c. Why wouldn't Jesus answer their question? _____

D. Summary: the greatest barrier to discipleship is the devil's continual tempting.

1. We want to grow and be a better disciple.
2. Satan continually tempts us to go backward and live for self again.
3. The disciple resists this temptation and goes forward with Jesus.

III. What do disciples do when they fail?

A. Repent

1. Repentance is turning away from sin.
2. Too many believe that admitting they are in sin is all there is to do. They think that once they admit sin, they may remain in it.
3. Many excuse sin by saying, "That's just how I am."
4. Excuses do not help us overcome failure but keep us locked in the patterns of sin.
5. Repentance includes the determination to stop sinning and is essential for the disciple who wants to overcome sin.
6. "But unless you _____ you will all likewise perish" (Luke 13:5).

LESSON 7 Disciples Fail but Never Quit

B. Confess.
   1. Confession is saying the same thing that God says.
   2. Before you were baptized, you confessed Jesus Christ as the Son of God. This was saying the same thing about Jesus that God says about Him, i.e. that He is the Son of God.
   ★ 3. Confession of sin is saying the same thing about sin that God says, i.e. that it is not right, causes a person to be separated from his God, and will cause people to be eternally lost.
   4. All attempts to rationalize away sin, blame others for it, or make excuses for what we have done run counter to the meaning of confession.
   5. Confession of sin is essential: "If we _____ our sins, He is faithful and just to forgive us our sins and to cleanse us from all unrighteousness" (1 John 1:9).

C. Pray
   1. Confession and repentance lead one to pray and ask for forgiveness.
   2. The Christian does not need to be baptized again and again after every sin because being a child of God gives one the right to pray and ask for forgiveness (1 Peter 3:12).
   3. Read the account of Simon the sorcerer in Acts 8:13-24.
      a. Was Simon a Christian?_____
      b. What was Simon's sin?_____
         _____
      c. What did Peter tell him to do about it?_____
         _____
      d. What did Simon ask Peter to do?_____
         _____
   3. Prayer is our powerful ally in overcoming sin: "Confess your _____ to one another, and _____ for one another, that you may be healed. The effective, fervent _____ of a righteous man avails much" (James 5:16).

D. Work on mastering temptation

1. Sin is not inevitable. We can improve our ability to conquer temptation.

2. We do this with a three part strategy:

   a. Controlling our desires—self control is all important. Read 2 Peter 1:5-10. Notice that self-control is a key link in the growth process that leads to "never stumbling" (verse 10).

   b. Limiting opportunities—read Genesis 39:7-13. Did Joseph flirt with Potiphar's wife, tease her, or otherwise constantly expose himself to temptation? _____

   ★ c. Praying for wisdom—read James 1:5. Will God give us the wisdom to defeat temptation? _____

3. God wants you to overcome sin and will help you. "No temptation has overtaken you except such as is common to man; but _____ is faithful, who will not _____ you to be tempted beyond what you are able, but with the _____ will also make the way of escape, that you may be able to bear it" (1 Corinthians 10:13).

4. Pray for God's help, look for the way of escape, and you can defeat the enticement of sin.

IV. Conclusion

A. Becoming a disciple does not mean we will never sin again.

  1. Just as Jesus' disciples did, we still fail the Lord.

  2. But through repentance, confession, and prayer we can be restored to the Lord to follow Him again.

B. This means one of the keys to Christianity is endurance.

  1. Do not allow yourself to become discouraged because you are not progressing as quickly as you want to or because you are still tempted to sin.

  2. Keep thinking about heaven and press on. Never entertain any ideas of quitting or not getting to heaven.

LESSON 7 Disciples Fail but Never Quit

3. Continue to work on mastering temptation and God will bless you. Trust Him and refuse to give up!

C. You have concluded the *Who Will Follow Jesus?* book. Discuss with the elders of the church or your teacher what materials you should study now. Don't stop learning and working on discipleship just because you have completed this material. Keep trying to be like Jesus!

www.ingramcontent.com/pod-product-compliance
Lightning Source LLC
Chambersburg PA
CBHW070452050426
42451CB00015B/3446